Tragic Fires Throughout History ™

The Great Chicago Fire of 1871

Christy Marx

The Rosen Publishing Group, Inc., New York

For Eric, Keaton, and Cat. Keep the home fires burning.

Published in 2004 by The Rosen Publishing Group, Inc.
29 East 21st Street, New York, NY 10010

Copyright © 2004 by The Rosen Publishing Group, Inc.

First Edition

Library of Congress Cataloging-in-Publication

Marx, Christy.
The great Chicago fire of 1871 / by Christy Marx.— 1st ed.
    p. cm. — (Tragic fires throughout history)
Summary: Describes the 1871 fire that destroyed much of Chicago, Illinois, examining its causes, the resulting devastation, and its aftermath.
Includes bibliographical references and index.
ISBN 0-8239-4487-5 (lib. bdg)
1. Great Fire, Chicago, Ill., 1871—Juvenile literature. 2. Fires—Illinois—Chicago—History—19th century—Juvenile literature. 3. Chicago (Ill.)—History—To 1875—Juvenile literature. [1. Fires—Illinois—Chicago—History—19th century. 2. Chicago (Ill.)—History—To 1875.] I. Title. II. Series.
F548.42 .M37 2004
977.3'11041—dc22

2003012447

Manufactured in the United States of America

CONTENTS

Introduction

On the evening of October 8, 1871, more than 300,000 weary residents of the great city of Chicago went to bed expecting nothing more than a quiet night's sleep followed by an ordinary Monday of going to work or tending to family. Instead, these unprepared citizens found themselves pursued by an inferno, driven into the waters of Lake Michigan or running far onto the open prairie north and west of the city. The people of Chicago were chased out of their city by one of the most destructive fires the world had ever seen.

The wall of flames roared and rumbled with a terrifying noise. Burning debris rose into the air on hurricane-like winds. The fire raced with such speed that it literally nipped at the heels of those who ran from it. The inferno destroyed entire buildings in minutes.

From the night of October 8 to the early morning of October 10, the Great Chicago Fire burned away nearly the entire city, claiming more than 2,600 acres (1,052 hectares). In the end, the Great Fire destroyed 18,000 buildings, from the humble shacks of the poor to the finest brick and marble homes of the rich.

The fire leveled banks, stores, hotels, railroad depots, courthouses, gasworks, waterworks, government buildings,

There was a rumor at the time that the Great Chicago Fire was started by an oil lamp kicked over by a cow. The rumor was further established by drawings and poems such as "The City That a Cow Kicked Over," which was written by Anna Matson and published in 1881.

newspaper publishing houses, opera houses, theaters, saloons, restaurants, insurance company buildings, schools, and churches—nothing could stand in its way. Enormous lumber mills, grain elevators, coal yards, breweries, warehouses, and factories of all kinds were burned to the ground. Priceless works of art, museums, and libraries were devoured. Countless numbers of pets, wild animals, and livestock were lost.

Amazingly, less than 300 people were killed in the fire. But afterward, more than 90,000 people were left without shelter, food, water, or anything more than the clothes they were wearing or the few precious possessions they managed to carry with them at the last minute.

People looked for someone—or something—to blame: foreign anarchists trying to overthrow the government; irresponsible firefighters who had been drinking; and, most famous, Mrs. O'Leary's cow who knocked over an oil lantern, setting the barn ablaze. None of these are true.

The sad fact is Chicago was a city that was just waiting to burn down.

The Queen of the West

What was destined to become one of the largest cities in the United States was first known to the Native Americans as Eschikagou, which roughly means "stinky-smelling place" or "land of the wild onions." It smelled bad because it was mostly swampland bordering the southwestern tip of Lake Michigan.

The first Europeans laid eyes on those marshes in 1673. But the man considered to be the true founder of Eschikagou was Jean Baptist Pointe du Sable, a trader from Haiti of mixed African and French-Canadian blood. He settled there in 1779 and soon established a successful trading post.

In 1803, Fort Dearborn was built on these lands, then later destroyed by Native Americans. It was rebuilt in 1816 and occupied by American troops for another twenty-one years.

Chicago officially became a city in 1837 with a population of 4,170. Newspaper reporter Frederick Francis Cook arrived in 1862 and he noted in his book, *Bygone Days in Chicago*, that the population was around 120,000. Only nine years later in 1871, the population had jumped to more than 330,000. Chicago quickly became a booming city.

The Garden City

By the late nineteenth century, Chicago had earned nicknames such as "the Queen of the West" and "the Garden City." Wide streets were lined with oak, maple, elm, birch, cherry, and hickory trees. A stretch of sandy marsh was turned into Lincoln Park at the edge of Lake Michigan.

Popular writer Sara Jane Clarke Lippincott described the city on July 12, 1871: "I see beautiful and stately marble buildings where four years ago were the humble little domiciles of the Germans, or the comfortless shanties of the Irish emigrants. What were then wastes of sand and rubbish and weeds are now lovely public squares or parks, with hard, smooth drives, ponds, rocks, hillocks, rustic bridges and seats, pretty vine-shaded arbors, and the usual park accompaniments of tame bears and caged eagles."

This was before electrical power. There were telegraphs, but no telephones. All vehicles including the streetcars were horse-drawn. Life moved at a slower pace.

The Three Divisions

Chicago is divided into several parts by a waterway called the Chicago River. The south and north branches of the Chicago River divide the West Division of the city from the eastern half that borders Lake Michigan. The main branch of the river cuts directly to the east forming a "T" shape, as it empties into the

This panoramic illustration from 1868 shows Chicago in all of its glory. Three years later, this city of more than 300,000 people would be reduced to rubble. In the center of this illustration is the Chicago River, which empties into Lake Michigan.

lake. This forms the dividing line between the North Division and the South Division. At the time, there were twelve wooden bridges over the branches of the river. The waterway and bridges would play an important part in people's flight from the fire.

The North Division

The North Division contained the fanciest, most expensive homes built by the city's original settlers, most of whom were now Chicago's rich, established families as well as political and

The limestone water tower and pumping station *(left)* that provided water for the city and the Rumsey House *(right)* were two of the most notable landmarks in Chicago before the 1871 fire swept through the city.

business leaders. The North Division contained the upscale neighborhoods near Lincoln Park and the tall, limestone water tower with the water pumping station. This single waterworks station pumped all of the water for the city, a fact that would later prove deadly.

The South Division

The South Division contained the heart of the business district and most of the city's government buildings. Its most prominent landmark was the imposing stone courthouse with its clock and 10,849-pound (4,049-kilogram) bronze bell in a wooden cupola at the top. There were also the gasworks, which pumped a type of natural gas used to provide light throughout the city. The Sherman House was a luxury six-story hotel built of marble. Crosby's Opera House had just been renovated and was scheduled to reopen one night after the fire began.

The West Division

The West Division contained lumber mills, factories, and a large Irish immigrant community. This was the poor side of town. Beyond the West Division, there was nothing but open prairie for miles and miles.

Fire Preparation

Chicago had seen fires before. A large fire in 1857 killed twenty-two people and led to the establishment of a professional fire-fighting force in the place of unpaid volunteers. Chicago averaged two fires a day, and there were twenty fires in the week leading up to the Great Fire.

According to the Chicago Historical Society, in 1871 Chicago had 185 firefighters "who worked in seventeen steam fire engine companies, six hose companies, four hook-and-ladder companies, and two hose elevator companies." These fire engines were horse-drawn. Additionally, a system of fire hydrants and fire alarms had been installed. Yet the city remained a terrible fire hazard for several reasons.

This photograph of one of Chicago's densely populated areas, taken before the fire, shows unpaved streets and sidewalks made from wooden boards.

Fire for Everything

All lighting, heating, and cooking required the use of fire. People used candles, oil lamps, kerosene lamps, wood shavings, coal, or gaslight—all of which provided a handy source of flames for accidents.

A City Made of Wood

Chicago was famous for its mud. When it did rain, the city streets turned to a mess of muck and mud. To deal with this, streets were sometimes paved with wooden planks or wooden blocks. Wooden sidewalks were elevated above the streets. According to *The Great Fire* by Jim Murphy, there were "over 55 miles [88 kilometers] of pine-block streets and 600 miles [966 km] of wooden sidewalks" throughout the city.

Drought

The spring and summer had produced little rainfall in Chicago, creating unusually dry conditions. Only a tiny amount of rain had fallen since early July, leaving wooden buildings dangerously dry.

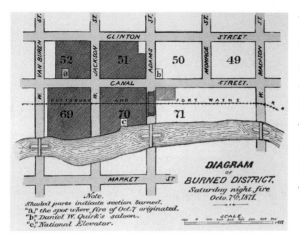

The night before the Great Fire, another fire burned in the city. It consumed four square city blocks, colored in here on this diagram. Half of Chicago's firefighters worked to put out the Saturday night fire, leaving them tired and ill-equipped to fight the fire that would destroy most of their city.

Although there were a few larger buildings made with stone or brick, the vast majority of the city's buildings were made of wood, especially in the poor sections where cheap wooden shacks were built close together. Worse yet, even the so-called fireproof buildings had wooden framework and wooden decorations. Nearly every piece of ornamentation that decorated these buildings was carved of wood, then painted to look like metal or stone.

Finally, most of the buildings were covered with wood shingles or tarred felt roofs that burned easily.

An Overworked Fire Department

Though the fire department had asked for many improvements, the city government ignored its requests. Instead of multiple water pumping stations, there was only one for the entire city. Much of the fire-fighting equipment was old and in need of replacement. To complicate matters, fire hydrants had been placed too far apart, and there weren't enough firefighters in the department.

THE PESHTIGO FIRE

By a terrible coincidence, the most deadly fire in American history also occurred on October 8, 1871, in Peshtigo, Wisconsin. While the Great Chicago Fire claimed around 200 lives, the Peshtigo fire took more than 1,500 lives. Yet the Peshtigo fire is mostly forgotten while the Great Chicago Fire entered history as a major event. The difference is that Peshtigo was an obscure lumber town, populated by nameless migrant workers whose deaths were overshadowed by the destruction of a rich, important city.

On Saturday night, October 7, there had been a severe fire in the West Division that burned down four square blocks. Half the entire force of 185 firemen battled the fire, suffering many injuries in the process. The exhausted firemen worked for eighteen hours to put out this fire and some of their equipment was damaged in the process. They had no time to recover.

The Final Deadly Element

Even with these other problems, the Great Fire might have been contained early on if not for the wind. On the evening of October 8, a violent wind began to blow from the southwest—the worst possible direction, for it would eventually drive the fire straight to the heart of the city.

Sunday, October 8

How sad and how strange are the memories now
Which hang round the heels of that old Leary cow—
That wretched old cow with the crumpled horn
That kicked over the lamp that set fire to the barn
That caused the Great Fire in Chicago!

— C. C. Hine, 1872

This excerpt of a poem entitled "Mrs. Leary's Cow," published in the *Insurance Monitor* shortly after the fire, shows how quickly the myth of Mrs. O'Leary and her cow entered the historical record. According to researcher-writer Richard Bales, the source of the myth came from an article in the *Chicago Evening Journal* on October 9, 1871, which reported the fire was "caused by a cow kicking over a lamp in a stable in which a woman was milking." This woman was quickly identified as an Irish Catholic immigrant, Mrs. Catherine O'Leary.

This explanation was quickly seized upon for two reasons. First, it provided a simple story to explain a terrible event. Second, it sprang from a strong undercurrent of prejudice against the Irish

ORIGIN OF THE GREAT CHICAGO FIRE OCT: 8th 1871.

FROM ORIGINAL PAINTING BY L.V.H.CROSBY

This caricature of Mrs. O'Leary by L. V. H. Crosby was one of many printed in the weeks following the fire. Although a number of factors were at the root of the fire, Mrs. O'Leary proved to be the most convenient scapegoat on which to pin the blame.

Catholic immigrants. Catherine O'Leary was afterward portrayed as a hideous old witch, a drunkard, a welfare cheat, and worse—for no other reason than her being poor and Irish.

Fact vs. Myth

The truth is the O'Learys were hardworking parents with five children. In *The Great Fire*, Jim Murphy wrote, "Both Patrick and Catherine [O'Leary] had to be up very early in the morning: he to set off for his job as a laborer; she to milk their . . . cows and then deliver the milk to neighbors."

Mrs. O'Leary testified at an official inquiry afterward, "I had six cows there. A good horse there. I had a wagon and harness and everything I was worth, I couldn't save that much out of it [snapping her finger], and upon my word I worked hard for them."

The O'Learys lived in a small cottage at 137 DeKoven Street and rented rooms in a front cottage to another family. The barn was a short distance from the cottages.

Who Did Start It?

During the official investigation, Catherine O'Leary testified that she and her family were all in bed by nine o'clock, though the people in the front cottage were having a party. It was two neighbors, Daniel "Peg Leg" Sullivan and Dennis Regan who discovered the fire, tried and failed to put it out, then woke the O'Learys and warned them. Of the animals inside the barn, only one calf was saved.

Ironically, the O'Learys' house survived the fire. This photograph of it from 1871 is entitled *The Scene of the Crime.*

17

In 1997, the *Illinois Historical Journal* published an article entitled, "Did the Cow Do It? A New Look at the Cause of the Great Chicago Fire," by Richard Bales. In the article, the author suspects Sullivan and Regan were behind the accident. Bales, who is an attorney, read the original testimony of Sullivan and Regan. He found many inconsistencies in their stories. According to Bales, it's likely that Sullivan and Regan were in the barn, perhaps smoking cigarettes, and caused the fire themselves with a carelessly tossed match. Of course, neither one was about to admit it!

There were 172 fire alarms, such as this one, placed around Chicago at the time of the fire.

The Great Fire Begins

However it happened, by 9:30 PM the barn was thoroughly ablaze and Patrick O'Leary was working desperately to wet down his own cottages so they wouldn't burn. Those two cottages did survive the fire.

The barn was filled with coal and straw that had been laid up for the winter. The powerful southwesterly wind picked up sparks and burning pieces of wood shavings and straw, and spread them to nearby buildings.

Joseph Edgar Chamberlin, a reporter from the *Chicago Evening*

Post, wrote, "I was at the scene in a few minutes . . . The land was thickly studded with one-story frame dwellings, cow stables, pig sties, corncribs, sheds innumerable; every wretched building within four feet of its neighbor, and everything of wood . . . " If swift action was taken, the fire might have been under control in its earliest stages.

A Series of Mistakes

In the cupola on top of the courthouse, a night watchman named Mathias Schafer spotted the signs of fire in the distance. He used a voice tube to call down the location of the fire to his assistant, William Brown, who then struck an alarm for the closest fire station. Unfortunately, Schafer told Brown to strike alarm box 342, which was a mile away from the right location.

THE FIRE EQUIPMENT

The fire engines of the time were horse-drawn carriages with large wooden wheels. The steam-powered engine, which would be used to pump the water out and fight fires, was introduced in the United States in 1852. The upright steam boiler forced steam through copper tubing. The steam powered a brass pump and pistons, enabling them to pump water under pressure. It was the latest in modern technology.

Not long after, Schafer realized his mistake. He called down for Brown to strike alarm box 319 instead, which was closer to the fire, but Brown refused to follow the order. He thought it would confuse the firemen.

Chicago instituted a professional fire department after an 1857 fire that resulted in the deaths of twenty-two people. The official fire department had only 185 firefighters, however—far too few for a city of Chicago's size.

Meanwhile, one of the O'Learys' neighbors ran to Bruno Goll's drugstore several blocks away. He told Goll to get the key for the fire alarm box in his store and sound the alarm. Goll supposedly refused to do so. Later, Goll claimed he rang the alarm twice. Either Goll lied or the alarm failed to work. No alarm from that box got through.

No matter what the reason was, there was a fatal delay before Engine No. 5 arrived at the scene—and then broke down!

The Firemen Meet Their Match

Members of a nearby hose company called the America had spotted the fire themselves. They arrived and attached their hoses to a hydrant eleven blocks away and began fighting the fire before more fire engines arrived. All of this took precious time. Horses had to be hitched to the fire engine wagons and the heavy leather hose had to be unrolled and laid out.

Meanwhile the fire gained strength. Spurred on by the wind, it jumped over streets and spread to more buildings. By now the fire was serious enough that Fire Marshal Robert A. Williams arrived at the scene. He sounded more alarms, but the engines had to come from miles away.

This hand-colored woodcut shows people trying to flee the city along the Chicago River as buildings burn around them. Paths along the river provided one of the safest refuges from the flames within the city.

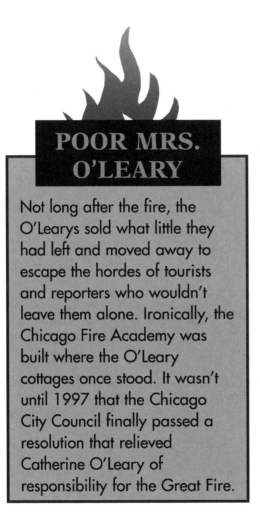

POOR MRS. O'LEARY

Not long after the fire, the O'Learys sold what little they had left and moved away to escape the hordes of tourists and reporters who wouldn't leave them alone. Ironically, the Chicago Fire Academy was built where the O'Leary cottages once stood. It wasn't until 1997 that the Chicago City Council finally passed a resolution that relieved Catherine O'Leary of responsibility for the Great Fire.

The flames raced to the east where they destroyed a church, then arrived at a match factory and a lumber mill. From this point on, the fire was completely beyond human control. On October 17, an article in the *Chicago Evening Post* read, "The firemen labored like heroes. Grimy, dusty, hoarse, soaked with water, time after time they charged up to the blazing foe only to be driven back to another position by its increasing fierceness, or to abandon as hopeless their task."

Out of Control

As midnight approached, vast quantities of combustible material fed the fire and the wind continued to carry burning sparks and debris through the air. The southern branch of the Chicago River was no barrier. The fire easily leaped the river and began to destroy the South Division.

Monday, October 9

By the early hours of Monday morning, shortly after midnight, a vast wall of flames raced to the east and to the north, devouring everything in its path. East of the river, it destroyed Conley's Patch, considered one of the worst southside Irish slums, filled with closely packed wooden shanties.

The fire was partially in check when it came to a line of freight depots. An eyewitness, Joel Bigelow, wrote in a letter to his family on October 10, " . . . the depots on the East side of track were also low Brick Slate roofs and no opening in the sides—this was a formidable barrier." A small section of the southernmost part of the city was left unburned because of this barrier, but that was the only piece of good luck.

The Gasworks

Soon people realized the fire was heading toward the gasworks. The gasworks supplied much of the city with natural gas—an extremely flammable substance—which was used to provide

The orange section of this map shows the swath the fire cut through the city, spreading across the Chicago River and along the bank of Lake Michigan. Mrs. O'Leary's house was located in the upper left-hand corner of this map.

light called gaslight. In a panic, people fled, getting as far away from the gasworks as they could. When the fire reached the gasworks, the area exploded, taking with it several surrounding buildings. The gasworks not only fueled the fire but also left much of the city without light.

Night Flight

By the early morning hours, thousands of people had been driven unexpectedly from their homes and into the night. Many witnesses described it as being caught in a snowstorm, except the "snow" was red sparks and cinders instead of white snowflakes.

"My coat had been on fire two or three times. People would run up to me and smother the flames with their hands. Then we hurried on, the fire madly pursuing us," wrote Bessie Bradwell, who was thirteen at the time. This brave girl kept calm even after being separated from her family. Her father thought she was dead until the night after the fire when he finally heard she had survived. During that whole time, Bessie carried to safety a heavy subscription book that was vital to her mother's publishing enterprise.

Eben Matthews, a bookkeeper, wrote in his recollection of the fire, "The fleeing crowd was increasing every moment and soon became a panic stricken one. A man came along dragging a trunk by the handle with one hand and leading a young child with the other. His wife had a small baby on one arm and a mirror on the other."

The Sherman House

The majestic Sherman House, a grand marble hotel, went down in flames so intense that some of the marble was reduced to powder. William Gallagher, a student at the Chicago Theological Seminary, wrote a letter to his sister on October 17 in which he noted with dark humor the comparisons to the legendary scene as Nero played his fiddle while Rome burned to the ground: "Theodore Thomas was at the Sherman House with his orchestra, and was to have commenced his concerts on the Monday night after the fire. He was compelled to run for his life, and leave some of the instruments, and some one wants to know why he is different from Nero. Answer: One fiddled away while his Rome was burning, and the other roamed away while his fiddles were burning."

The Randolph Street Bridge

Hundreds, if not thousands of people, made for one of the few intact bridges leading to the West Division where the fire had not yet reached. The *Chicago Evening Post* reporter, Joseph Chamberlin, wrote: "A torrent of humanity was pouring over the bridge. Drays, express wagons, trucks, and conveyances of every

This illustration captures the scene of a mass exodus of people crossing the Randolph Street Bridge as the fire rages in the background. The fire would destroy the homes and possessions of hundreds of thousands of city residents. Many of the people who fled the city would have nowhere to go back to the next day.

conceivable species and size crowded across in indiscriminate haste. Collisions happened almost every moment, and when one overloaded wagon broke down, there were enough men on hand to drag it and its contents over the bridge by main force."

One of the stranger sights Chamberlin saw was a group of boys hired by an undertaker, carrying a line of wooden coffins on their backs across the bridge, no doubt anticipating they would be needed.

The Courthouse

At the height of the blaze, the huge bronze bell on top of the courthouse rang for five hours, sounding the alarm. Schafer, the night watchman who spotted the fire, found himself busy fighting airborne cinders that kept landing on the wooden cupola, but it was a losing battle. The cupola was in flames and he escaped by sliding down banisters to the lower floors.

There was a jail in the basement of the courthouse and the prisoners were set free. Moments later, the massive bell finally crashed down through the building and into the basement. After the Great Fire, this bell was melted down to make tiny bells that were sold as souvenirs.

A Rude Awakening

The fire continued relentlessly eastward across the South Division, then headed north where it jumped across the main branch of the Chicago River. There the fire began a destructive rampage across the North Division, where huge grain elevators went up in fiery explosions.

People awoke in the middle of the night to the frightening noise of the fire and its eerie orange glow. Some people had enough time to drag furniture out into piles on the street, hoping to save it somehow. Instead, the furniture simply got in the way of the fire engines or the people trying to escape, and eventually it became more fuel for the fire. Others paid outrageous prices to anyone with a wagon to carry off their possessions to the north or west away from the flames. But most people barely had enough time to throw on clothes and run with their arms filled with whatever precious possessions they could manage to carry.

Anna Higginson wrote a letter to friends on November 10, 1871, in which she said, "The wind, blowing a hurricane, howling like myriads of evil spirits drove the flames before it with a force & fierceness which could never be described or imagined; it was not flame but a solid wall of fire which was hurled against the buildings & the houses did not burn, they were simply destroyed."

The Waterworks

At the edge of Lake Michigan, in the North Division, stood the waterworks, which supplied much of the city with water. At first, water had continued pumping to the city and many people poured water onto their homes trying to save them.

But around 3:00 AM, the fire reached the waterworks. The tall water tower built of limestone resisted the fire, but the actual pumping engines were across the street. Eben Matthews, a bookkeeper who escaped from the South Division, wrote, "All of this part of the city could have been saved had not the waterworks been burned earlier in the night. A temporary roof has been put on the waterworks pending a new and fireproof one. This roof caught fire early in the morning and the timbers partially burned fell on the pumping machinery putting it out of commission."

With the waterworks gone, all hope was lost. Now the doomed city had no source of water. There was nothing left to do but run.

The *Chicago Tribune*

Editor Horace White of the *Tribune* was proud of his newspaper and the Tribune Building, which was considered to be one of the city's new "fireproof" constructions. During the night, he went to the office where his staff managed to publish an emergency edition about the ongoing disaster. He left feeling secure that his building would withstand the flames.

But his building had one terrible flaw—a wooden roof with a layer of tar on top of it. His employees kept the roof wet until the water stopped, then tried to stomp out the windblown cinders as they landed. Eventually the fire won, and the employees ran to escape. The great fireproof building was gutted to the ground, leaving behind a shell of blackened stone walls.

29

Back home, White and his family loaded as much as they could onto a wagon, piling on trunks, suitcases, a hamper of food, and even a pet green parrot. His home and his newspaper building both went up in flames.

Seeking Escape

There were only two ways out for the rest of the city—east to the shores of Lake Michigan or out onto the prairie to the north.

On October 15, William H. Carter, a commissioner on the city's Board of Public Works wrote a letter to his brother: "The flames were rushing most frantically, leaping from block to block—whole squares vanishing as though they were gossamer. Men, women and children rushing frantically in all directions to save their lives—some away—but others into traps and places where they were soon surrounded and no retreat left. Hundreds rushed upon the shore of the lake where they had to hug the beach and waters until the flames subsided, giving them a chance to escape."

As the fire kept coming, people had to abandon what they'd carried with them and leave it in piles on the shore while they waded out into the cold water of the lake. Some people tried throwing water on their possessions, but the heat was too intense. The shivering, water-soaked survivors had to watch everything in sight burn to ashes before them.

Chicago residents gather amid the tombstones of a cemetery located in the southern end of Lincoln Park. The fire would eventually spread through here, damaging crypts and monuments.

Some of the boats on the river and lake caught fire as well. Barges burned up at the docks. The wind blew sparks that set fire to the tall, wooden masts of the sailing ships at anchor.

Lincoln Park

Farther to the north, the same scene was played out in Lincoln Park on the edge of the lake. The fire raged right through an old cemetery in the south end of this park where many soldiers from the Civil War were buried, burning down wooden grave markers and stone vaults alike. But the open area of the park proved a safe haven for the thousands of people who found themselves trapped there on the edge of the lake for long, terrifying hours as they waited for the fire to burn itself out.

Here, equality was enforced upon the citizens, as the richest citizens found themselves alongside the poor working-class immigrants. They were left with one thing in common—the fire burned everything they owned.

The Best and Worst of Humanity

As the fire roared on with nothing to stand up against it, both the best and the worst sides of people were brought out. In some parts of the city, men broke into saloons and went on drunken rampages of looting. Grown men yanked pathetic bundles of belongings from the hands of children or stole wagons filled with goods. People ran in panic, knocking over and trampling anyone in their way. Some people with wagons took cash to carry someone's possessions, only to go a few blocks, toss off the belongings, and find a new victim to fleece.

In other places, people remained calm and behaved in an orderly manner. Firemen ignored their own burning homes as they battled to save someone else's house. Kind strangers took care of lost children or banded together to help one another. Good-hearted men like the seminary student William Gallagher hurried ahead of the fire, helping people escape and even helping them carry their possessions away from homes about to burn.

This illustration of men breaking open casks of liquor appeared in several newspapers. Although most city residents were concerned for their safety, others engaged in looting and drinking sprees while the city burned.

North Division Burns

Halted by Lake Michigan to the east, the fire continued unchecked to the north. The main road, Lincoln Boulevard, was clogged with people and wagons desperately fleeing the flames.

One of them was Julia Lemos, who worked as an artist. She single-handedly had to guide her four children and baby, sick mother, and elderly father to safety. They managed to transport a large pile of their belongings onto the prairie, only to have the fire catch up to them there, burning across the long, dry grasses.

Rush Street Bridge *(far right, opposite page)* is overwhelmed by the number of people running from the flames. The fire gutted the few brick structures in the city, leaving nothing standing but the skeletons of charred buildings. This devastated landscape *(right)* was once Chicago's business district.

Once again they had to flee, farther out onto the prairie, leaving behind everything they'd struggled to save. Lemos wrote in a later account, "I had to wake the children up, and we had to run again, and leave everything to burn, this time we felt the heat on our backs when we ran, like when one stands with the back to a grate fire."

Outrunning the fire, they pulled boards off an old fence to use as a sleeping area and laid down in exhaustion. As it grew dark, a heavy rain began to fall and once again they ran, this time finding shelter in a shed at a farm. Their only good fortune was that a policeman had found and buried Julia's father's two precious trunks of belongings, and these managed to survive the fire.

The Late Rain

Though it arrived too late to do much good, the heavy rain that fell late Monday night was blessed by the survivors of the destroyed city. It helped to dampen and slow what remained of the fire. By the early morning hours of October 10, the fire was all but over. The Queen of the West was in ruins.

Tragically, this same rain brought misery and death to hundreds of people who had been chased onto the open prairie where they had no shelter or heat, and most had no clothes to spare. Many died of exposure to the elements during the cold, wet night. At the same time, it was estimated that around forty babies were born on the prairie where thousands had taken refuge.

Aftermath

Around 2:00 AM on October 9, the mayor of Chicago, Roswell B. Mason, sent desperate telegrams to the closest cities. His message read, "CHICAGO IS IN FLAMES" and asked for help. According to *The Great Fire* by Jim Murphy, several cities—from Milwaukee, Wisconsin, to Pittsburgh, Pennsylvania—sent aid during the fire's aftermath. By Tuesday, much of the nation as well as other countries had learned of the disaster, and already the first trainloads and wagonloads of food, clothing, and other aid poured into the city. Toys came from Paris. England helped build a new library. Altogether, Europe donated a million dollars.

It was two days before the ruins of the city cooled down enough for survivors to take stock of what remained. Eyewitnesses reported amazing sights, such as melted metal wheels and the iron rails of the streetcars curled up in the air. Giant heaps of coal continued to burn for weeks.

Francis Test wrote in a letter to his mother on October 13, "The iron safes stood the heat well, but many were burned to a white heat; their contents were destroyed. I can safely say over two thirds of them were found to contain nothing but charred masses of what once were thousands in bonds and notes." Other eyewitnesses reported that when safes were opened, the heat was so great that the papers inside burst into flame when exposed to air.

Lieutenant-General Philip H. Sheridan was highly regarded as a hero for the order he imposed upon the city in the aftermath of the fire. Of Sheridan, Test wrote, "General Sheridan has control here now and this has done much to stay the confidence of the people. He is a little God here. The city is not strictly under martial law but it reminds me of the first days of the rebellion [the Civil War]. Soldiers march our streets; the citizens are patrolling the squares; every alley is guarded and woe be to him that lights a match or smokes a cigar on the street after nightfall." Most of the 450-man police force had lost their homes, so about 5,000 men were sworn in as a temporary police force called the First Regiment of Chicago Volunteers.

Recovery

In the immediate days and nights that followed, there was no forgiveness for looters, some of whom tried to start new fires. Looters caught in the act were shot on the spot or dragged to the nearest lamppost and hanged.

Church basements were converted to hospitals and shelter for the homeless. General Sheridan had hundreds of army tents pitched in the parks and prairie. Executive orders were issued that

The members of this family pictured in this woodcut are doing their best to live in the charred remains of their home. Although relief and aid came pouring into the city, it took years for things to return to normal.

set a reasonable price for bread and other food, banned smoking, limited the hours of operations in saloons, and forced wagon drivers not to charge excessive fees.

On October 14, James W. Milner wrote in a letter to a friend, "The general sentiment and feeling of the people is an honor to humanity. The business men are cool and cheerful. A quiet determination to accept the situation, and steadily weather it through to better times, is the prevailing feeling."

Beginning on October 13, administration of the city was turned over to the Relief and Aid Society, formed specifically to deal with the tragedy and losses. It saw to the distribution of food and clothes, donated materials for rebuilding, gave smallpox vaccinations, and provided money to those in need. Its work lasted for the next three years. While its efforts were far from perfect and were affected by social and class bias, there's no doubt it provided vital relief in a time of crisis.

Mary Kehoe, a working-class girl of sixteen at the time of the fire, wrote in a memoir to her granddaughter in 1942, "The relief & aid society built barracks of rough lumber in Washington Park for the people to live in. Two rooms for families. A new kitchen stove and the usual kitchen things and anyone could get a new Singer sewing machine just for the asking."

Immediately following the fire, one of the most urgent needs was for water. A pair of locomotives provided power to pump some water from the lake into tanks. The tanks were driven around the city on wagons and water was handed out. It took weeks to repair the pumping engines of the waterworks, and when they first began to work again, the water was stagnant from sitting in the pipes too long. The bad water caused a wave of severe illness.

Eventually, all these hardships were overcome and the city slowly began to recover. It was a bumpy road of rebuilding, marked by economic troubles and a second fire in July 1874 that burned another 800 buildings. After this second "Little Fire," as it was called, the city finally changed some of its building regulations to require more fireproof construction.

On the twenty-fifth anniversary of the fire in 1896, newspaper journalist George Warrington Steevens described an enormous

This illustration is part of a special section issued by the Chicago paper the *Inter Ocean* on October 9, 1893, the twenty-second anniversary of the fire.

parade that lasted for five hours: "By their untamable energy they have built her up from a heap of ashes in their own lifetime to be great and wealthy and pulsing with virility. Not if I had a hundred tongues, every one shouting a different language in a different key, could I do justice to her splendid chaos." It took many years, but Chicago had reclaimed her title and was Queen of the West once more.

Timeline

(All times are approximate).

Saturday, October 7, 1871

10:00 PM
A large fire burns four square blocks in the West Division, leaving many firefighters exhausted or hurt.

Sunday, October 8, 1871

9:00–9:20 PM
A fire breaks out in the O'Leary barn.

9:20–9:40 PM
The first alarm sounds Box 342, sending the fire company to the wrong location.

9:40–10:00 PM
More fire companies arrive to fight the fire, which has now spread to several buildings and is out of control.

10:00 PM–12:00 AM
Bateman's Lumber Mills burn. The fire jumps across the south branch of the Chicago River. Around midnight, the gasworks explode and Conley's Patch burns.

Monday, October 9, 1871

1:00 AM
The fire reaches and destroys the Palmer House Hotel as it burns eastward across the South Division.

1: 30 AM
The courthouse burns down.

2:00 AM
The Sherman House burns.

2:00–4:00 AM
The fire leaps across the main branch of the Chicago River and rages into the North Division, as well as continuing eastward across the South Division.

3:00 AM

The water pumping station burns, leaving the city without water.

4:00–6:00 AM

The fire chases desperate people to the edge of Lake Michigan.

6:00–8:00 AM

William Ogden's huge lumber yard, a railroad complex, and the McCormick Reaper Works are on fire. Enormous grain elevators along the north bank of the Chicago River burn down. Residents in the North Division are pushed farther onto the prairie.

8:00–10:00 AM

The only remaining bridge into the South Division is the Twelfth Street Bridge. The North Division is still burning. People clog Lincoln Avenue as they attempt to get out of the red hot city to the safety of the northwestern prairie land.

10:00 AM–Noon

General Sheridan has homes along Michigan Avenue blown up in an attempt to stop the progress of the fire to the south.

Noon–6:00 PM

People continue to flee the fire raging through the North Division.

6:00–midnight

As night falls, a short, hard rain finally brings relief to the burning city, but it causes terrible misery to the thousands of homeless people on the cold, open prairie.

Tuesday, October 10, 1871

The first relief and emergency supplies begin to arrive from other cities. The city is still too hot for most people to return to the burned sections. Fire continues to burn in isolated areas, such as smoldering coal heaps.

Glossary

anarchist (AN-ar-kist) A person who seeks to overthrow established society or government by violent means.

cupola (KYOO-puh-luh) A small construction on a roof.

freight depot (FRAYT DE-PO) A railroad warehouse used for storing and shipping merchandise.

gossamer (GOSS-uh-mur) A lightweight cobweb or extremely thin and delicate material.

grain elevator (GRAYN EL-ih-VAY-ter) A large silo where grain is stored.

hillock (HILL-ok) A small hill.

hook and ladder (HOOK and LAD-dur) A wagon that carried long ladders, hooked poles and other firefighting equipment.

hose company (HOZ CUM-pan-ee) A team of men who supplied hoses to other companies of firefighters during a fire.

looting (LOOT-ing) To take money or goods by force.

scapegoat (SKAPE-GOHT) A person who is made to take the blame for others, or to suffer in place of someone else.

stagnant (STAG-nant) Not flowing or moving.

steam engine (STEEM EN-jin) Usually an engine in which a sliding piston in a cylinder is moved by the expansive action of the steam generated in a boiler.

For More Information

Chicago Fire Academy
558 West DeKoven Street
Chicago, IL 60607
(312) 747-7238

Chicago Historical Society
Clark Street at North Avenue
Chicago, IL 60614-6071
(312) 642-4600
Web site: http://www.chicagohs.org

National Fallen Firefighters Foundation
P.O. Drawer 498
Emmitsburg, MD 27171
(301) 447-1365
Web site: http://www.firehero.org/

Web Sites

Due to the changing nature of Internet links, the Rosen Publishing Group, Inc., has developed an online list of Web sites related to the subject of this book. This site is updated regularly. Please use this link to access the list:

http://www.rosenlinks.com/tfth/gcfe

For Further Reading

Bales, Richard F. *The Great Chicago Fire and the Myth of Mrs. O'Leary's Cow*. Jefferson, NC: McFarland and Company, 2002.

Cowan, David. *Great Chicago Fires: Historic Blazes That Shaped a City*. Chicago: Lake Claremont Press, 2001.

Gillem Robinet, Harriet. *Children of the Fire*. New York: Aladdin Library, 2001.

Lowe, David. *The Great Chicago Fire: In Eyewitness Accounts and 70 Contemporary Photographs and Illustrations*. New York: Dover Publications, 1979

McClelland, Paul. *The Great Chicago Fire, October 8–10, 1871, Described by Eight Men and Women Who Experienced Its Horrors*. Chicago: Chicago Historical Society, 1971.

Sawislak, Karen. *Smoldering City: Chicagoans and the Great Fire, 1871–1874*. Chicago: The University of Chicago Press, 1995.

Bibliography

Bales, Richard. The Chicago Historical Society. "Did the Cow Do It? A New Look at the Cause of the Great Chicago Fire." 2001. Retrieved April 7, 2003 (http://www.chicagohs.org/fire/witnesses/library.html).

Chicago Historical Society. "The Great Chicago Fire and the Web of Memory." 1996. Retrieved April 7, 2003 (http://www.chicagohs.org/fire/witnesses/library.html).

Milner, James. "An Anthology of Fire Narratives." October 14, 1871. The Chicago Historical Society. 1996. Retrieved April 2003 (http://www.chicagohs.org/fire/witnesses/library.html).

Murphy, Jim. *The Great Fire*. New York: Scholastic, Inc., 1995.

Nova. "Escape: Because Accidents Happen: Fire." Transcript 1999–2002. Retrieved April 7, 2003. (http://www.pbs.org/wgbh/nova/transcripts/2604fire.html).

PBS. *American Experience*. "Chicago, City of the Century." 1999–2003. Retrieved April 7, 2003 (http://www.pbs.org/wgbh/amex/chicago/maps/chicago_fire_text.html).

Smith, Dennis. *Dennis Smith's History of Firefighting in America: 300 Years of Courage*. New York: Doubleday, 1980.

Test, Francis. "An Anthology of Fire Narratives." October 13, 1871. The Chicago Historical Society. 1996. Retrieved April 2003 (http://www.chicagohs.org/fire/witnesses/library.html).

Index

About the Author

Christy Marx has written for television, film, animation, computer games and comic books. Amongst the shows she's written for are Babylon 5, Twilight Zone, He-Man, and others. Her other books for Rosen include biographies of Jet Li and Admiral Grace Hopper, and a book on The Ocean Depths. Christy lives in California with her lifemate and a horde of cats. Visit her Web site at www.christymarx.com.

Photo Credits

cover, pp. 1, 5, 10, 12, 13, 16, 17, 18, 20, 24, 31, 40 Chicago Historical Society; p. 9 © Royalty-Free/Corbis; p. 21 © North Wind Picture Archives; pp. 26, 38 Bettmann/Corbis; p. 33 Special Collections and Preservation Division, Chicago Public Library; pp. 34, 35 Milstein Division of United States History, Local History and Genealogy, The New York Public Library, Astor, Lenox and Tilden Foundations.

Designer: Les Kanturek; Editor: Charles Hofer; Photo Researcher: Amy Feinberg